THE PIECES OF MY PLATFORM

A Collaboration Presented By:
Living The Life I Love, LLC

The Pieces of My Platform

Copyright © 2017
Stevii Aisha Mills
&
Living the Life I Love, LLC

Cover Design By:
Mr. Duane Nash
designnash@gmail.com

All Rights Reserved.
This book or any portion thereof may not be reproduced or used in any manner whatsoever without the express written permission of the publisher, except for the use of brief quotations in a book review.

Printed in the United States of America

ISBN 13: 978-0-0991837-3-1

Unless otherwise stated, all references to The Holy Bible are taken from these versions:
King James, New King James, and New International.

SBG MEDIA GROUP, LLC
Atlanta, Georgia
www.thescatterbrainedgenius.com/publishing

ACKNOWLEDGEMENTS

Karen Mills, Momanger: Thank you for helping to truly put together the pieces of my platform. I love and appreciate you.

Fred Mills, Daddy: Thank you for showing me strength, tenacity, and purpose this year. Your songs continue to flow through me.

Duane Nash: God placed you in my life 20 years ago, and He continues to bless me by having you still here. I thank you for all that you do and all that you are.

Dr. Marilyn Porter and SBG Media Group: Thank you for always seeing me!

Authors of *The Pieces of My Platform*: Thank you for enclosing your words in the pages of this book. May your platforms continue to flourish. I love y'all!

FOREWORD

Many times in life, we fall in love with the big picture and do our best to overlook the pieces that create the picture. As a visionary, I totally understand. I naturally see the big picture first, and in a strong and vibrant way. I have learned to value the pieces. They are the elements that engage us into the experience. Without the pieces that I have had that no one wants to hear about (and I have not always wanted to talk about)—molestation, rape, homelessness, abortion, identity issues, rejection, and more—I would not have the powerful platform I have today. I would not be able to appreciate the pieces that other applaud: having a graduate degree, being a full-time entrepreneur since 2009, and working with celebrities and influencers.

Today, I am blessed to be a sought-after Speaker, Host of The Conversation with Stevii podcast which airs on iHeart Radio, Public Relations Consultant, and an International Best-Selling Author.

This book, *The Pieces of My Platform*, allows you a front row seat into the testimonies of powerful women I have had the honor to have in my 'I Love My Life Ambassadors' program this year. They have overcome the odds and have used their pieces to strengthen their platforms. The amazing this is that we overcome by the testimonies of others. I cordially invite you to be empowered, inspired, educated, and motivated as they take you on their journeys so that you can ascend to dominating yours.

Love,
Stevii

www.stevii.com

MY 2017 PLATFORM
Stevii Aisha Mills

- 'The Conversation with Stevii' was approved to be aired on iHeart Radio.
- Made a 5-figure income in the first eight months of 2017.
- Switched from 'Done For You PR Services' to PR Consulting primarily.
- Traveled with my live event, 'Experience!', to Roanoke, Virginia; Fulton, Maryland; and Atlanta, Georgia.
- Created the 'I Love My Life Ambassadors' Community with 58 paid members.
- Created the 'I Love My Life Ambassadors' Intensive with 10 women.
- Hosted the 'Shift' Telesummit.
- Awarded the 'It-Factor Award' at The Featured Highlights Award.
- Elevated my credit score over 600 points.
- Interviewed for Shade Y. Adu's 'Build Brand Bank It' Summit.
- Worked as a substitute teacher for Roanoke City Public Schools.
- Started a relationship with a phenomenal man.
- Asked to return to the 'Social Media Dream Team' for Cheryl Wood.

- Hosted 'Pink and Purple Footprints' to celebrate survivors of Domestic Violence and Breast Cancer.
- Spoke on the same stage as Lisa Nichols.
- Increased the fees for my services.
- Coordinated *The Pieces of My Platform* anthology.
- Became an Amazon International Best-Seller.
- Became a qualified representative with World Ventures.
- A highly sought-after Speaker for virtual and live events.
- Bonus: I literally fell and got back up in all aspects of my life.

TABLE OF CONTENTS

ACKNOWLEDGEMENTS VI
FOREWORD VII
MY 2017 PLATFORM - STEVII AISHA MILLS VIII
THE BUILDING BEGINS… 1
PAIN, PRESSED, PROSPERING 3
    LaTonya Knox 3
FROM FEAR TO FAVOR 9
    Carol Craven 9
PIECES OF FAITH LED ME TO FULFILLMENT 15
    Ti'Keya Lawrence 15
YOU ARE MORE THAN ENOUGH 21
    Alicia E. Diggs 21
NOT WATERED DOWN 28
    San Griffin 28
FROM INCARCERATED TO INPOWERED 35
    Min. Kiesha L. Peterson 35
NEVER ABANDONED 42
    Wendy Magee 42
MY SOMEDAY IS TODAY 50
    Dr. Min. Mary Faison 50
FROM TRAGEDY TO TRIUMPH: MY LIFE OF FAITH 56
    Pastor Cassandra Elliott 56
PRESSURE BUSTS PIPES 62
    Tawana T. Valentine Sampson 62
ABANDONMENT 69
    Montell McClain 69

ALL OF THE PIECES WERE NECESSARY	76
Cynthia Randolph	76
SPONSORS	80
THEIR FACES	85
PLATFORM BUILDER: STEVII AISHA MILLS	86
PLATFORM BUILDER: PASTOR CASSANDRA ELLIOTT	87
PLATFORM BUILDER: CYNTHIA RANDOLPH	88
PLATFORM BUILDER: MARY FAISON	89
PLATFORM BUILDER: LATONYA KNOX	90
PLATFORM BUILDER: TI'KEYA LAWRENCE	91
PLATFORM BUILDER: ALICIA DIGGS	92
PLATFORM BUILDER: SAN GRIFFIN	93
PLATFORM BUILDER: MINISTER KIESHA PETERSON	94
PLATFORM BUILDER: WENDY MAGEE	95
PLATFORM BUILDER: TAWANA T. VALENTINE SAMPSON	96
PLATFORM BUILDER: CAROL CRAVEN	97
ABOUT THE VISIONARY AUTHOR	99
STEVII AISHA MILLS' ACHIEVEMENTS	101
APPENDIX	102

The Building Begins...

LaTonya Knox is a native of South Carolina. Born and raised in the small town of Hemingway, she now resides in the beautiful city of Myrtle Beach. She is a woman of faith, a wife, and mother of two beautiful children. She is a Style Strategist for busy professional woman, a Speaker, and an International Best-Selling Co-Author of the book *Leaving Our Legacy*. She is the Founder of Diamond Beauty by LaTonya C. Knox, LLC and PowerUp International, an organization created to help women who are affected by adversities of the system (incarceration, rehabilitation, domestic abuse, homelessness, etc.) to restart their lives anew. Her mission is to share her story in hopes that she can give women the strength to push through obstacles to become women of empowerment.

PAIN, PRESSED, PROSPERING
LaTonya Knox

One day, as I was watching one of my favorite TV series Flash, the main character (played by Barry Allen) kept going back in time trying to change the past in the hope of saving someone he loved. The first thing I thought was, "If I could go back in time, would I change anything?" Without hesitation, my answer was "NO!" Everything I have experienced, everything I have done—good and bad, right or wrong—has shaped and formed me into the woman I am. And I love the woman I am. But let me be honest with you: It hasn't always been this way. There was a time I wished…oh, did I wish…I could go back in time and rewrite history. I lived a life of regrets and allowed my past to put me into a prison of unforgiveness of myself.

I have never shared my entire story with anyone. Many have heard stories or some aspect of what I may have shared, but never have I ever allowed myself to be 'naked with my truth'. When people meet me, they tend to think of me as shy, meek, and sometimes timid. If they only knew why I am the way I am today. I once was an angry, sad, depressed girl who held her emotions in. I manipulated others, lied to others, played victim, and lived a life of hatred within. I covered it well. But, as we all know; volcanoes will erupt. Let me tell you: I erupted over 10 years ago. All that I felt, all that I endured—it all erupted, landing me in a place I would never wish on anyone, friend or enemy.

My life is what I describe as a journey of pain, pressing, and prospering. My pain began when I was raped. I never felt such pain. I never felt such embarrassment. I never felt such guilt and shame. I felt as if I had disappointed those who love me. I felt like I disappointed myself. But I didn't sit on it. I reported it to the police and followed protocol. Still, the feelings of hurt, distrust, anger, and sadness would not leave me. I went to counseling, and yes, it helped—for what it was worth. But it took most of my life for me to understand that I wasn't at fault. I didn't have to live a life of shame. Most importantly, I had to learn that I couldn't live a life of distrust.

Then, there was my family life. It was not the greatest, but I survived. My mom: A woman of strength, integrity, and honesty. A woman after God's heart. A praying woman who, no matter what we were going through, made sure I stayed in God's Word. I thank her for making sure I never departed from God. She did everything she could to keep me protected, to love me like Jesus. Even after all I have done, she never left my side. She always remained proud of me. She never gave up on me. She was and still is my 'Jesus'. She was my first encounter with Jesus. My mom and I are as close as a mother and daughter can be…maybe even closer. She is my rock. And when I saw my dad trying to take her away from me, my entire life flashed before my eyes! All I could think to myself was, "How could I go on without her if he succeeded in his efforts to take her life?" But GOD made sure that didn't happen, and I am grateful and blessed to have this woman here with me. This event caused me to feel anger—a rage I never felt in my life. And you know what? At that time, it felt good. I wanted to hurt anyone and everyone who crossed me. I didn't care about anyone else's life. I didn't even care about my own life. I just wanted someone to feel what I felt, and it didn't matter who it was.

Twice I tried to take my life. First, with pills; the second time, with a gun. That latter caused me to go to jail. Yes, you heard me right. In the eyes of man and the system, I am a felon. And this is where the pressing began. Before I went to jail, I went to a mental institution where I stayed for about a month. I did the daily medication and group counseling routines. I was a zombie there. Honestly, I barely remember what occurred. Once I passed the evaluations, I went to jail for 2 ½ months. And when I say, "God kept me", He kept me.

Here I was: This 100-lb. woman in jail with women who committed all sorts of crimes. One had killed her significant other and became my best friend there. Who would have imagined that this meek, quiet, and shy girl would have ended up there? Well, I did. I had allowed all of my hurt, pain, and anger to take control of me. I completely lost control. BUT GOD kept me. God kept me safe and protected. I was covered by the blood of Jesus. Thank you, Mom!

Let me back up for a moment and talk about the first time I tried to commit suicide with pills. That is a moment I remember as if it were yesterday. I was lying in bed and I heard the voices of the enemy say, "You are causing everyone pain" and "Nobody loves you". But he did not stop there. He kept on talking: "Do everyone a favor and go away forever." "Why are you still here?" "Do you think God loves you?" And he kept on talking, saying, "You are a waste of space, energy, and body. Everyone hates you. You keep causing your mom pain. Just die already!"—AND THAT was enough for me to take a bottle of sleeping pills. BUT GOD!!!

When I laid down and closed my eyes, I heard God's voice. He loudly said, "NO!" I wasn't sure I heard Him, but He repeated once again: "NO! I AM NOT THROUGH WITH YOU YET!" It was so loud, I thought the world heard it, too. But no; just me. I woke up—let me rephrase that. I JUMPED UP out of my bed, went to my mom, told her what I'd done, and we booked out of there to the hospital. My eyes were wide open; I just couldn't close my eyes! When I got to the hospital, the doctors were very surprised to see me so awake and alert. Most people who attempt suicide by ingesting pills are usually unconscious and need to have their stomach pumped. I just drank the charcoal (which was disgusting, by the way). They were very surprised at how articulate I was and how I was able to explain what I was feeling. So, of course, the protocol after that was to go to counseling. I did that for a while. It seemed like everyone just wanted to medicate me. God made it very clear He didn't want me under the influence. He wanted me to be able to hear His voice, so I declined the medication.

Let's fast-forward to my incarceration. I was scared. I cried. I did not know why I allowed the enemy to control me. I do not regret it, though. It was the most transformational experience I have ever had. God used an inmate as my protector, meaning I never had to worry about being bothered or hurt by anyone. God used the guards as my covering. They made sure I was safe all the time, and anyone who tried to hinder that safety was removed from my cell. As I sit here writing, I am smiling because I am now realizing I was supposed to be there for such a time as that! That was no happenstance. God used me to be their first encounter with 'Jesus'.

The stories I could tell would be endless, but I will save those for another time. I do want to say this, however: When I walked into the courtroom before the judge, she said, "You don't belong here. I just believe you got off track and lost your way. I am going to send you back out and I want you to be the woman I know God has called you to be". BUT GOD!!! I saw the angels surrounding me in the courtroom at that moment, and I knew my Heavenly Father was there.

Today, I am here writing this chapter of my story because I want you to know that you never, EVER be too low for God to reach you. If I can make it through the pain, past the pressing, and into the prospering, SO CAN YOU!

Carol Danielle Craven is the third and youngest daughter of Colen and Bertha Craven. Originally a North Carolina native who now resides in Maryland, she is a proud mother of four and a college graduate of the illustrious Shaw University with a B.A. in Religion and Philosophy. She is the business owner of Southern Comfort by Carol, a southern-style catering service in New Carrollton, Maryland. Carol treasures her relationship with God, her family, and her blossoming entrepreneur activities. She believes when women come together, contribute and pour into each other with honesty and integrity, amazing things can happen for their immediate communities and for the world. Carol believes when women are fully-committed to their cause and what they were created to do, they become socially-responsible for the growth and potential to make the world a better place.

FROM FEAR TO FAVOR
Carol Craven

I am going to share my testimony of faith and favor! A testimony deep and rich with a plethora of intense emotions and convention. A testimony that only God could render favorable. I can only start from a place of fear and brokenness. We can't have a testimony without a test!

As you read in my bio, I am a graduate of Shaw University with a Bachelor's in Religion and Philosophy. I am also the Owner of Southern Comfort by Carol, a southern cuisine-based catering service in New Carrollton, Maryland. I am a mother of four, an avid reader, and a support of entrepreneurship for women in business. I believe when we share our gifts, others are inspired and empowered to share their gifts. There is nothing more powerful than when women come together with the intentions of uplifting and encouraging one another.

My journey from fear to favor is intertwined with ups and downs, losses and gains. I have learned through different experiences that you can't have bitter without sweet and joy without pain. Some of my greatest gains have come from times that were difficult and heavy. My life wasn't always that map of clarity and destination that it has become. I had to learn endurance and perseverance. Next to grace and mercy, endurance and perseverance taught me how to hold on, pray, commune with my Creator, and value what God placed in me to contribute to the world. I had the tools and potential, yet I had no idea that tragedy and the vicissitudes of life would define who I would become. Who would have known everything I would go through to become happy, whole, and secure would come from loneliness, pain, and feelings of doubt?

I always knew I had a powerful spirit and force within me. It is my belief that most people want to share their happier experiences to motivate others. That takes less commitment and responsibility. Sharing the good times of our lives can be just as fleeting as the moment. It is also my belief that when we tap into those candid moments when we have experienced pain, our purpose has an opportunity to live.

My empowering moment of transition to led me to the DMV (District of Columbia/Maryland/Virginia) area didn't come from planning. It wasn't the reward for completing my B.A. and being 13 classes away from completing my Master's. It did not come from the amazing meals I am now able to provide as a caterer. My move came from losing everything I had, coupled with the willingness to leave a painful past in North Carolina—trusting completely that God knew what was best for me and allowing Him to create a tailor-made experience I was assigned to have. I did not know what the transition would lead to, but I knew it had to be greater than the pain I had already experienced.

A little less than two years ago (from the time of this writing), I arrived in New Carrollton, Maryland, broke and broken. I had my teenagers (who were devastated about the move) in tow, and only $230.00 in my pocket. All of my despair and heartache were now being released into the hands of my best friend who graciously took us in. Her ability to give to us from a place of love and stability ultimately set the course for the joy I now hold! It was not easy to move from all that I had ever known, but it was imperative that I honored God and allowed myself to be in position for what was to come. I had to be in position to surrender, be vulnerable, and open.

The events that led to this journey were hard. I had to face all of my demons. I lost my job, my home, and my savings was depleted. Beyond the thought of going to a shelter, I had nowhere to go. No one in my life in North Carolina at the time was in position to assist. During this time, I also ended up in the hospital with multiple health issues, which placed me out of work, leading to the loss of my position. At the time, I discovered that my mind and body were exhausted. I understood that I needed and deserved a game-changer. I needed a change in my life so powerful that I would KNOW it was help from God. My best friend urged me to come to Maryland. She helped me understand that what I needed was an impactful opportunity, not a bail out. I needed to get my affairs in order.

The first two months were very difficult. I had to update my resume, apply for jobs, work on rebuilding my credit, and learn how to drive in DMV traffic! The driving alone had me begging God to snap His fingers and immediately make everything alright. But in that eight-week timespan, there was a shift in my spirit. Life was happening, I was on the move, and my confidence was soaring. Within six of the eight weeks, I was hired for three positions (which I firmly secured) and accepted two. I began to work excessively on paying off debt, fixing my credit, and aggressively saving money every week. I was beginning to understand that God had not forgotten about me. He had a marvelous plan! My responsibility was to show up and respond accordingly!

There are so many details I wish I could share to render the value of that move, but I only have this chapter—for which I am eternally grateful! What I have learned is that in order to grow, sometimes you have to GO! The Word teaches us that a prophet is not without honor, except in his hometown, among his relatives, and in his own household (Mark 6:4). It was with this knowledge and principle that I was able to transition my life, continue my education, renew my mind, get my finances in order, and start a business. I needed to be reminded of my grace, beauty, and intellect.

I was "trapped" in North Carolina because no one understood what God created me to do. My life now in Maryland has afforded me the opportunity to understand that a butterfly cannot be held. The pain I endured in my 'cocoon process' prepared me for the freedom to express my priceless beauty and self-worth.

The situations we experience in life are to provide growth and wisdom. Never run from your pain and hard times. Stand strong in the face of adversity and grow fierce! The wisdom I have gained from trusting God is immeasurable. I would not have the joy and peace I now have without my journey and the pain I had to endure. I am grateful for everything I have experienced, and now I can share from a place of wisdom to the tribe I have been assigned to witness to.

As I bring this chapter to a close, I am honored to have been given this opportunity to share this part of my life. Being open and willing to share will always elevate you to the next level. Always remember: There is purpose in your pain. God will never let your experiences be in vain. We have all been called to usher in the Spirit of God and to share how mighty He is in our lives. Share, my Sisters! Share! We never know the impact our experiences will have on the sisters who have been assigned to us. Never be afraid to share those hard times. My hard times are the core of who I am today. I am living in my truth and sharing my passion for life through the ministry of my business.

It is my heartfelt hope that I have encouraged just one person who reads this to stay the course and stay focused. Your life will open up and develop as you become more willing to seek God's face and walk in His alignment.

Now, move forth in your assignment and be encouraged. The world needs your input and impact!

Ti'Keya Lawrence made a courageous decision to take on full-time entrepreneurship and resigned from her job as a Paramedic after almost 18 years. She loved being a Paramedic in one of the busiest cities in the country, but it had run its course in her life and she was destined to do more. Ti'Keya is the mastermind behind *Love M.E.E., LLC*. The brand's mission is to motivate, empower, and encourage women on self-love. Her brand pillars are: Self-Awareness, Inner Peace, Happiness, and Good Health. Ti'Keya resides in Maryland with her husband. Learn more by visiting her website: **www.lovemeellc.com**.

PIECES OF FAITH LED ME TO FULFILLMENT
Ti'Keya Lawrence

It is amazing how fear will really deceive you. Fear will come in and paralyze you to the point where you think you cannot move and so, you do not. It is one of the worst feelings in the world to feel stuck, especially for an ambitious person like myself. When we come into the world, we are fearless because we have not experienced any of the harsh realities that life entails.

I remember being about 10 years old. I was riding my bike near my house and fell off, cut my chin wide open, and had to get six stitches. From then on, I seldom rode my bike because I was afraid of falling. As you go through life, different things will happen to cause you to become fearful, leading you to a place of feeling stuck and paralyzed. While my friends would be outside on their bikes, I would not join them. It took many years for me to get over the fear of riding a bike again. Notice I said "again". I did eventually get past the fear. I even enjoy bike-riding now, especially when I go on vacation.

When I started my career as an EMT, I was so happy to be doing something in the medical field where I would be helping people. That's all I've ever wanted to do! I was so excited to have accomplished something by being certified and then obtaining my good government job in the city where I grew up and lived most of my life. My ambitious nature had me wanting to do more. Within two years, I became an EMT/Paramedic and was able to do even more for the patients I would interact with. In my opinion, at some point, the job's mission got off track. I no longer felt the light burning inside of me anymore. I felt terrible about the place I was in. It did not feel authentic and I found myself uncomfortable when it came to my job.

I had already made the decision to further my education by obtaining a college degree, but I wasn't sure which direction I wanted to go. After pursuing nursing a few times, I finally concluded that business would be the degree of choice. The light came back on! I had a new goal to accomplish and be proud of! Along with my love for helping people, I had an entrepreneurial spirit I knew would one day provide a means for me to be in business. In 2009, I graduated with my degree. I had been in my career for 10 years at the time, which is the amount of time chances of burnout can set in for a Paramedic. I considered that heavily and how it may affect my health and happiness. A decision had to be made. I often considered leaving the job to go into business, but I had no solid plan; so, I waited and contemplated. Contemplation was then questioned: Was I operating in fear?

As life would have it, things happened. The country faced The Great Recession, my relationship fell apart, and I drove myself into a bout with depression. With everything happening around me, it was not an ideal time to change careers. My faith had to step in and take over. I had to believe God was not done with me yet. There was much more for me, and I had to snap out of that depressive state. I motivated myself to pull it together and have faith that I would be fine. I had no choice but to believe that and operate 100% in my faith. I figured out how to deal with the overwhelming things the recession had brought about with being an Owner of several properties. I trusted God totally, as far as my relationship and whatever man I was supposed to marry, and I pressed forward.

My next challenge was to practice some patience and figure out a plan to leave my job. I wanted to step out on faith to be in business and a full-time entrepreneur. That had been my desire for many years, but I didn't take that leap. I had to realize why fear existed. I had no clue of what it would be like stepping out on my own, not receiving a check every other week, and not having a career to fall back on—just in case things didn't go how I anticipated.

Eventually, I reached a point where I could not take it anymore. I had to figure my way out of the situation. I found myself almost feeling depressed again. I got very honest with myself and had to face my reality: I was scared to leave my job and its security. I also had to face the unfulfilled feelings I struggled with that could have led me back into a state of depression. I decided I was going to set a date and would do everything I needed to do to follow through with it. I was determined.

I have always worked on my faith to build it up and keep myself believing the Word of God for my life. I had to realize that doing so would always be a part of life's journey. I got to the point of saying, "I trust God. I know I am going to be taken care of. I will be fine".

I began to diligently work on my plan, and a few things came to mind—one which of the utmost importance. I asked myself, "In what ways can I continue to help people?" That was my heart's desire. That is what I loved to do. I became really focused, got deep into the Word, and stepped my faith up to the max. I believed I could figure out things, just as I did before. I operated in faith with the decisions I made. I had to put into play those same methods I used when I was overwhelmed during the recession; trusting God on marriage and pulling myself out of being depressed. I did what I needed to do and started a new business that would fulfill my desires in helping people. I was ready to soar!

The paralysis was no more and is long gone. The main thing I needed was my faith to fall back on to keep me going, direct me, and assure me that everything would be okay. Once I started to walk in that direction, things started to fall into place. My platform began to come together, and I could see things happening. I resigned from my job and put myself in a position to be able to succeed, as long as I believed I could and kept my faith.

I started to meet other business owners, brand builders, influencers, authors, coaches, and speakers. I surrounded myself with those people and opportunities started to present themselves, such as being a co-author in this book. I have participated in other endeavors, and my determination to live a life I love will remain a priority for me. Once again, I have that feeling of fulfillment by not being fearful and stepping out on faith. The glow inside of me is back, and I love every minute of it! At this point, I am fulfilled with the direction my life is headed.

Everything I am experiencing is meant for me. I believe God's will for my life and will always show up and achieve. My faith is strong and I refuse to believe anything other than that. I will remain in that faith, stay believing, and trust God. God never fails. We must have faith and stay strong in that faith. I am just getting started, and I know there will be things that will happen beyond my imagination just by trusting God and letting Him lead the way.

Being able to share messages about love to women on loving themselves and having enough love to share with others is important. Ultimately, that's what Jesus Christ wants us to do: Love others as we love ourselves. These are the pieces of my platform and the things that have all come together in my life to create my declaration of on love of self and others. We ALL have an innate desire to be loved. We can start with loving ourselves SO much, that it pours out of us into others. This kind of love has no fear and fulfills so many purposes. I truly hope that all who read this book know the depths of true love—a love that comes from God—the love of self, and how sharing that love will impact all of our lives.

Alicia E. Diggs is a native of Philadelphia, Pennsylvania, a mother, a grandmother, and the Author of *Standing on My Healing: From Tainted to Chosen*. She is a Public Speaker, Activist, Advocate and Educator for HIV/AIDS, and has recently received the 2017 'Dorothy Height Human Rights Award'. Alicia has a Bachelor's Degree in Social Word from the University of North Carolina at Greensboro, a Master's Degree from Capella University in Minnesota, and is a Doctorate candidate also with Capella University. She is also the CEO and Founder of *I will Live*, which is a Foundation created to educate, motivate, and empower others to live healthy and productive lives. **Alicia E. Diggs is the voice for the voiceless!**

YOU ARE MORE THAN ENOUGH
Alicia E. Diggs

Some of us had a pretty good childhood; some of us had a challenging childhood. I grew up in the suburbs of Philadelphia, Pennsylvania in a household that was beautiful on the outside, but was actually hell on the inside.

My mother suffered severe physical and verbal domestic violence by the hands of my stepdad for 10 years. Seeing physical violence should not be the norm for a child, but it was for me. When children are growing, they should be surrounded with love, encouragement, and protection. As much as my mother tried to give those things, there was interference by her abuser.

For the most part, I stayed in my books and participated in school activities. Those things helped keep my mind off of the problems that occurred in the household. As I grew into a teenager, I was pretty naïve and extremely afraid of males because of what I saw at home. I always thought that if you didn't do what a man told you, he would beat you. Some of my friends were into boys and even had boyfriends, but I was too afraid of that. Plus, my mom was not going for me having a boyfriend. I was a friendly and fun teenaged girl with several friends I loved to spend time with.

I spent lots of time with one particular friend I called my 'sister'. At the tender age of 13, I was taken advantage of by her 19-

year-old uncle on several occasions. I did not tell anyone because I was afraid he would hurt me, even though he was always nice to me—aside from the sexual abuse. I also knew my mom would be very upset. By the time I was 14 years old, I became pregnant by that guy and later had an abortion. By the age of 18, I was pregnant again, but this time I planned it with my new boyfriend who I just KNEW was going to be my husband. That dream was short-lived, so I became a single parent. By the age of 22, I had my second child by a man who threatened my life if I did not stay with him.

Going through those different mishaps in my life, I became pretty depressed much of the time. I hit it with smiles and laughter when I was around people. As I was growing into a young girl, a teenager, and then a woman, I had low self-esteem. I simply did not like the person I was. I always felt like I was not good enough for anything or anyone. According to the National Institute of Mental Health (2016), "Depression (major depressive disorder or clinical depression) is defined as a common but serious mood disorder. It causes severe symptoms that affect how you feel, think, and handle daily activities, including sleeping, eating, or working." Many of us go through depression and do not even realize that some of the things we do and say are a result of depression. For me, I normally responded to episodes of depression by eating, withdrawing from others, drinking, or even having sex with men I knew did not love or want me. Many times, I felt rejected by people and stigmatized because of my complexion, body build, and the fact that I was a single mother. I wanted to feel loved and accepted, even if that meant belittling myself to activities that were not in my best interest (let alone healthy) for me.

Eventually, I moved from Philadelphia, Pennsylvania to North Carolina to start a new life and create some stability for my children. In doing so, I was able to build a relationship with my biological father and rededicate my life back to God. Over time, I started to learn who I was as a woman and the things I could do to be a better woman and mother without the feelings of rejection, stigma, and unworthiness. I worked full-time, went to school, and made a vow to wait for my husband and not have sexual relations with anyone until I got married. Through my waiting, I rekindled a relationship with my high school sweetie whom I had known since I was 14 years old. We married in 2001. Two months after, on December 13th, I received the diagnosis of HIV. I was separated from him in less than six months after he boldly told me to my face that he knew he had AIDS and didn't care that he infected me with HIV. By 2004, I was happily divorced.

That was a journey I was not prepared to travel, BUT GOD! During those dark times, I had to really learn to speak life into myself and build a relationship with God. I knew I could not give up because what I also knew was that what the enemy meant for my bad, God would always turn around for my good. I made a decision for me that I wanted to live, and I WILL LIVE! I began to surround myself with people who not only spoke life and encouragement into me, but also who mentored and helped me in realizing my strength. I posted words of encouragement throughout my home where I could see them constantly. I spoke uplifting words into my own life, even when I didn't believe them. I allowed God to show me how beautifully, fearfully, and wonderfully made I am, which made a big difference in my life.

Overcoming the shame I felt about the things I had to deal with over time, plus sharing my life's stories with others, have allowed me to be set free from all of the hurt I endured in the past. As a woman living with HIV, the stigma that has existed since the beginning of the HIV epidemic swarmed me like it did others in the HIV community. In hopes of minimizing the stigma and the feelings of rejection and unworthiness, I made it a point to thoroughly educate myself so that I could help educate others. Stigmas hurt people and cause them to be divided from other persons and populations. Webster's Dictionary (2017) defines stigma as, "A scar left by a hot iron; a mark of shame or discredit; and identifying mark or characteristic; specifically, a specific diagnostic sign of a disease".

Listed below are some facts from Avert.org (2017):

- HIV-related stigma and discrimination refers to prejudice, negative attitudes, and abuse directed a people living with HIV and AIDS.

- In 35% of countries with available data, over 50% of people report having discriminatory attitudes towards people living with HIV.
- Stigma and discrimination also makes people vulnerable to HIV.
- Those most at risk to HIV (key affected populations) continue to face stigma and discrimination based on their actual or perceived health status, race, socioeconomic status, age, sex, sexual orientation or gender identity, or other grounds.
- Stigma and discrimination manifests itself in many ways. Discrimination and other human rights violations may occur in healthcare settings, barring people from accessing health services or enjoying quality health care.
- Some people living with HIV and other key affected populations are shunned by family, peers, and the wider community, while others face poor treatment in educational and work settings, erosion of their rights, and psychological damage. These all limit access to HIV testing, treatment, and other HIV services.

I took a stand to not only advocate for myself, but for others who experience stigma because they are 'different'. Everyone deserves to be treated with respect and dignity, regardless of their health status, race, socioeconomic status, size, age, sex, sexual orientation or gender identity, or other differences. I encourage and empower as many people as God places in my life by helping them to not be afraid, embarrassed, rejected, or stigmatized.

God will not put more on you than what you can bear. When God made you, He broke the mold because you are extraordinary and one-of-a-kind! You are perfect in His sight and He loves you unconditionally.

Stand tall with your head held high and your shoulders back, full of confidence because YOU ARE MORE THAN ENOUGH!

San Griffin is a skilled professional in Child Development and Family Relations, with over 15 years of experience working with youth and their families. Upon receiving a Bachelor's Degree in Child Development and Family Relations and a Master's Degree in Human Development, both from North Carolina Central University, her mission is to educate, inspire, and positively impact families around the world. Griffin, a wife and mother of three, takes this mission seriously. As CEO of her brand, Aggrandize Your Life, LLC, Griffin uses her love of the brain and mind (neuroscience) to coach aspiring entrepreneurs to master their brain's creativity, emotions, and productivity to reach their highest level of success. The Aggrandize Your Life brand also offers early education workshops for adults approved for North Carolina DHHS credit hours and entrepreneur and empowerment workshops for youth of all ages, in conjunction with school and college tours. Connect with her at: www.aggrandizeyourlife.com.

NOT WATERED DOWN
San Griffin

> *"They tried to bury me…they didn't know I was a seed."*
> ~ Mexican Proverb ~

I have had individuals be deceitful and misconstrue the truth regarding me. Have you ever felt like it was a campaign to discredit you and ignore your very existence? Have you entered a new level of progress and suddenly be faced with an increased animosity and an intense change in the atmosphere when you are around certain people?

Let me be the first to tell you: YOU are extremely SPECIAL and have a unique purpose in life. Why would there be such a campaign against you? Arm yourself with a smile and galvanize! Keep moving. Continue to aim for your goals and, most importantly, serve people. My mother, the late Patricia Taborn, would often remind me, "There is always someone worse off; therefore, be grateful where you are and help someone in need". When you submerge yourself in helping others, whether volunteering in the community, in your church, or a non-profit organization, you lose yourself in something that is bigger than you. Listen: We all have some sort of dysfunction going on, okay? However, you are unique! Random-thought alert. There's a study that reveals people who smile a lot see the world differently. In fact, they feel the world is smiling back at them. Therefore, I urge you to not allow negative people to steal your smile!

I want to share a recent WIN with you regarding The Pieces of My Platform. A couple of years ago, I experienced a very arduous, transformative time in my life. I achieved a major academic goal and financial blessing. The tides started to turn, as if I felt honorary; when in fact, I just desired to be spoken to decently, welcomed, and not ignored. Due to the unflinching love I have for myself, I had to acknowledge and remove myself from that harmful culture. This left me alone in various areas, including my family's nonprofit.

I observed this island culture, which seemed to chase me from the time I was a child. I felt isolated, harnessing feelings of loneliness and disconnect from my tribe. I realized there is power in belonging, power in unity, and power in numbers. Consequently, though much prayer and supplication, I was empowered to network, keep going, set goals, and find people 'like me'; people who wanted to network, do good things, and just enjoy life. You know…people who don't sweat the small stuff and think BIG! However, I went from being somewhat introverted to being a mediocre extrovert. I caught hold of the KEY and its people!

In retrospect, most of my introverted feelings derived from being hurt by people or witnessing insane behaviors. I turned inward instead of outward. Oftentimes, life hurts us so bad, we put up walls. Those very walls keep out pain, but they also keep new joys from entering. So, what did I do? I blasted down the wall! I prayed and asked God for direction. The words verbatim were, "Lord, if you want me to continue to operate this nonprofit and continue our annual Young Entrepreneur Expo, You must send me help. I know I can't do this alone".

To make a long story short, that particular year was our best with the community and in media, with the highest number of volunteers ever! Two magazines and two newspapers reached out to us, and we were featured in three out of the four. The two magazines highlighted me as the Director along with the agency, subsequently starting my branding and giving me fuel to persist. There's nothing wrong with being rewarded or being celebrated. I'm telling you this because I want you to know I had to tell myself that, too.

The culture that was created around me had me afraid to celebrate myself or allow others to do the same. Initially, I actually told one of the magazine owners that my bio didn't have to be included in the article—unless it was needed to fill more space. I was nervous about what people were going to say. "Who does she think she is?" or "Why did they highlight HER?"—all negative chatter we entertain in our minds at times. Actually, you should celebrate milestones! It will indeed propel you to your next goal!

According to neuroscience, when you reach a milestone, your brain releases a feel-good chemical called Dopamine. Do you remember how good you felt when you received that diploma, certification, or degree; something you were in the grind for and you were finally able to see the light of day? You felt that Dopamine release! (This new journey thrusted me into my newfound love for neuroscience. I gave you that 'nugget' for free.) Yes! That Dopamine is what helps us stay in the game; the game of LIFE!

I digress. Back to the story...

Truly humbled by the articles that highlighted me as the Director of the nonprofit and the agency as well, I couldn't help but think about the handful of folks who didn't want to acknowledge my mere existence. Now, people across the state and the world were reading about me. These magazines had digital platforms in addition to traditional hard copy publications. The Young Entrepreneur Expo was also fruitful. We had Gold Sponsors, support from businesses in the community, over 10 volunteers, and a host of young entrepreneurs and community supporters at the annual event. In fact, it was the first year we were able to give out 100 free swag bags to the first 100 youth who participated! Needless to say, the event was a success!

In addition, a descendant of my family from the west coast reached out to me that same year. She was in my state and looking to connect. She became a wonderful support to me, the family, and all of my endeavors. Of course, I was ecstatic and grateful. God was connecting me with the people connected to manifesting my destiny.

I am sharing my true story to tell you this: Please don't waste time trying to water yourself down. BE YOU!

Know that hurt people, hurt people. Unfortunately, that's what they do. Know when it is time to elevate your circle. You need people. So, keep networking until you find the right cohorts, associates, or partners. You could be one person away from that million-dollar networking opportunity. Let rejection be a sign to motivate you, not a sign for you to stop. Prior to the networking, I put my goals on a vision board and wrote in my journal daily.

I am a prolific, awe-inspiring workshop presenter, among other things. I presented my first workshop that summer with a group of youth and parents. As I networked and shared its success with associates, invitations started to come in. This happened without me advertising as I had planned. Things started to move fast! Be careful what you ask for; you will attract it!

My favorite quote is:

Preparation + Opportunity = Success

I was relatively prepared, and the rest is phenomenal history!

Finally, as of today, I call all of you reading this book, this chapter, HEPHZIBAH and BEULAH (biblical Hebrew names). That's the word God gave to me in the beginning of 2017. It means favored, married, and fruitful. Remember: I was battling feeling like an island all alone. He vividly urged me to read Isaiah 62:4.

Yes, people: In the context of business, my workshops are awe-inspiring and favored. Upon connecting with several pertinent groups, the opportunity to pen this chapter became available. Truly humbled, I took the moment to bless you and encourage you to seek collaborations and be joined together in a business context if you feel like an island. Yes, I am fruitful. The opportunities are multiplying, even as you read this very sentence. There is a benefit in being linked to professional women who are seeking sisterhood and pursuing goals without being intimidated by the sister beside them. Just like a flower garden, we are all blooming, beautiful, and unique.

Most importantly, the relationships mentioned in the beginning of my story have been restored. There are just a few snippets of the pieces of my platform. The pieces of your platform are unique situations and circumstances that have thrusted or guided you to where you need to be, to become who you need to be, and to add value to the world. There will be some unappealing seasons, but understand they are preparing you to relate, reflect, and release on a phenomenal level with your tribe and the people you are destined to touch.

I wish you all the same success: Favor, divine connections, and fruitful unions! I call you Hephzibah and Beulah! Truly!

Kiesha L. Peterson is a mother of three, an Amazon Best-Selling and Amazon International Best-Selling Author, an Ordained Minister, and an Internet Radio Show Host. She is a Co-Author of *Stories from The Pink Pulpit: Women in Ministry Speak!* and a self-published Author of *Knowing When Enough is Enough: My Guide to Building Your Self-Esteem; Book of Poems: Vol. 1;* and *I Am Who God Says I Am* under the pen name G.C. Peterson. She is currently working on her fourth book entitled *Be the Best You You Can Be*. She once served as Administrative Assistant to former Assemblyman William D. Payne. She also has an Associate's Degree in Criminal Justice from Everest University. Kiesha is a proud member of Alpha Generation Ministries, The Pink Pulpit, Silver Life Member of NAACP Tri-City Branch, National Council of Negro Women, Women's Speak Association, International Sisters Strengthening Sisters, and The Soul Restoration Center.

THE PIECES OF MY PLATFORM

FROM INCARCERATED TO INPOWERED
Min. Kiesha L. Peterson

How often have you been told to "leave your past in the past"? How often have you been made to believe that your past will dictate your future? Well, I want to encourage you to remember your past! Use your past as a valuable learning tool.

I reflect on my life daily, and I'm reminded of so many things God has brought me through. One incident was when I was incarcerated at the Middlesex County Correctional Facility in North Brunswick, New Jersey. It all started after I had gotten married. That right there was, in itself, the first mistake. Now, don't get me wrong: I don't regret getting married. I loved my husband and, through that union, I gave birth to my oldest daughter. However, he was not the husband God had for me.

I worked for an insurance company as a Clerk Typist in Workmen's Compensation. My responsibilities included generating claim checks for the injured. One day, my husband and I were talking about what I did on my job. From that discussion, the lame idea was devised and birthed: For claimants with the same name as his, I would generate a check in his name and send it to his mother's house. It worked for a while—until he was caught cashing the checks. My husband was arrested because he had a criminal history. I was fired, but God's favor was still on me in the mess! My employer showed compassion towards me because I had two minor children at the time and, subsequently, I was given probation since the crime was a first-time offense.

Not only did I lose my job, but I couldn't afford the apartment we had. After periods of moving to live with my stepdad and my husband's aunt, we finally found a place of our own in Newark, New Jersey after my husband was released from jail. Along with the child support I received for my son, welfare and food stamp assistance from Essex County helped with the rent and food. I was blessed to find a job as a receptionist at the YMCA in Orange, New Jersey. I don't remember even having received my first paycheck from them before the Essex County Sheriff's Department showed up.

I still laugh about that day today. Before they said anything, I knew exactly who they were when they walked in. I hadn't been able to keep up with my probation appointments in New Brunswick. Back then, I didn't think to have the appointments transferred to Union or even closer in Newark where I was living at the time.

So, as the officers walked up to the desk—a black woman and white man—I smiled and extended the greeting. "Welcome to the YMCA. How may I help you?"

The woman smiled back and said, "We are looking for Kiesha Peterson."

I just laughed and said, "I am she."

The Human Resources office was right across the hall from my desk and had to be notified that I was being taken. The woman asked if she had to put the handcuffs on me. I told her, "No, I'm too big and it is too hot to be running from anybody."

When we arrived at the Essex County Jail, she had to handcuff me because of protocol, but she put my hands in front of me and covered them with my jacket. I was sad, hurt, and a bit confused. The background check for my apartment came back positive, which is how I could get the apartment. Yet the background check done by the YMCA was the one that was flagged.

I was moved from Essex County to the Middlesex County jail because the violation and warrant for my arrest had been issued out of New Brunswick. I wasn't nervous, but I kept praying, "God, I'm sorry. Please keep me covered". As soon as I was able, I called my husband and told him what happened. I had to calm him down and give him instructions on what to do with my son and daughter. My son went to live with his dad. My aunt kept my daughter. Although he was my daughter's father, my husband was not in any shape to take care of her because he had become addicted to cocaine.

Let my oldest sister tell it, my husband snitched on me to get his time reduced. It really didn't matter to me, though. I felt I could now get the situation take care of and out of my life. Eventually, I was sentenced to 18 months in the Middlesex County Correctional Facility. It wasn't as bad as I had imagined it would be. The women were very respectful after they met me. Even the Correctional Officers said I must have made a wrong turn at the top of the hill because I looked so out of place.

I know it was the grace of God that allowed me to get out and into a program called ISP (Intensive Supervision Program). I knew I had to go through that to be a testimony for someone else. I thanked God every day for bringing me out and for keeping me safe. After I was released, I was able to go to my old school, Essex County Training, Inc., and get a part-time job as a Teacher's Aide. During that time, I became an Office Assistant (intern) for 10,000 Mentors, located right down the hall from where I worked. From there, I obtained a full-time job as a Clerk Typist with Rutgers College of Nursing—all while on ISP. Just before graduating from ISP, I was given the opportunity to work for then newly-elected Honorable William D. Payne, 29th Legislative District Assemblyman, as his Administrative Assistant.

Even after all the doors God had opened for me, I still allowed the views of others to dictate how I was to live my life and who I was to become. I was made to think I was 'less than' because I had been incarcerated. I became promiscuous. I started sleeping with a married man, letting myself think it was okay because I knew for a fact his wife was cheating on him.

Then, one day, I heard God call my name and tell me it was time; time for me to live the life He called me to live, to be the woman

He needed me to be. He needed me to tell the story of how I was incarcerated for three months for violation of probation, and that I was on probation because I had been convicted of embezzling money from an insurance company I had worked for. I was told I would not be able to get a good job after being incarcerated. Not only was I able to work for Rutgers University, I also became the Administrative Assistant to the now-former Assemblyman, William D. Payne, who, to this day, is a well-known New Jersey State Legislator. He was the Assemblyman who implemented the Amistad Legislation.

I realized despite all the mistakes I had made, God had forgiven me. I just needed to learn how to forgive myself and keep it moving. My mother taught me that I should treat people the way I would want them to treat me. I know with that and God's help, I have been able to overcome what they say about people who have been incarcerated. We have the power to make life good or bad. We can go left or right. It's all about our attitude and outlook on things.

There's an old song called "Life is What You Make It" by Leon Patillo. It says, "Life is what you make it; it is all up to you. Life is what you make it; all of your dreams can come true". It's all about what we say 'yes' and 'no' to. It's all about agreeing with the positive and disagreeing with the negative. God has given us the ability to make choices for ourselves, whether right or wrong. We have the ability and the knowledge to know the difference. My niece once told me that we are our own worst critics.

WE must STOP being our OWN roadblocks and learn how to be our OWN BRIDGE TO SUCCESS. ATTRACT the POSITIVE and REPEL the NEGATIVE!

Wendy Magee has been married to David Magee, Jr. for 10 years. They have two beautiful children: Kaleb and Kyrie. Wendy was born and raised in Port Arthur, Texas. She obtained her Bachelor's Degree in Criminal Justice at Wiley College and her Master's in Human Services. She currently resides in New Orleans, Louisiana. In 2016, Wendy self-published *And She Called Him Lord*. She believes when people begin to understand God's purpose for marriage, it will provoke them to live an UNbelievable life that will compel people to investigate the power of God for a divorce-proof marriage. In 2017, Wendy started "Speak Up" Ministry, where her focus is to lift up marriages and relationships through edification and empowerment. Wendy enjoys spending time with her family and working with young adults through her husband's non-profit, H.Y.P.E. She attends Mount Carmel Ministry and is an Ordained Minister under the leadership of Apostle Arthal Thomas, Sr.

NEVER ABANDONED
Wendy Magee

As I look over my life, God has allowed me to make choices that didn't physically kill me, but were detrimental to my spirit. *"All things are lawful [that is, morally legitimate, permissible], but not all things are beneficial or advantageous. All things are lawful, but not all things are constructive [to character] and edifying [to spiritual life]."* (1 Corinthians 10:23, AMP).

Like many young women, I dreamed of a beautiful wedding and marrying the man of my dreams. Little did I know: Marriage is deeper than two people saying "I do". I met my husband at a youth conference. We dated long distance for three years and then married. Early into our marriage, I had trust issues which stemmed from past experiences. My husband gave me no reason not to trust him, but I allowed my past experiences to taint my view of him.

Years passed, and I began to let down my guard. I started listening to secular music and not feeding my spirit godly things. I was angry all the time and constantly argued with my husband. My anger and lack of trust began to drive a wedge in my marriage. What I imagined I wanted in my dream marriage led to my creating a nightmare. In the nightmare I created, I began to look for attention outside of my marriage. I knew it was wrong, but I felt justified…because my guard was down. When you begin to walk in the flesh, you will reap the flesh.

"I say then: walk in the Spirit, and you shall not fulfill the lust of the flesh. For the flesh lusts against the Spirit, and the Spirit against the flesh; and these are contrary to one another, so that you do not do the things that you wish. But if you are led by the Spirit, you are not under the law."

(Galatians 5:16-18, NKJV)

Immediately, I felt broken. I knew I did wrong and I felt unworthy of God's and my husband's love. I told my husband, our Pastor, and family what I had done. Little did I know that my husband was entertaining someone else in 'conversation'. I thought, "What have I done? I've pushed my husband away. I don't hear from God. My family believes I'm untrustworthy..." I was broken, hopeless, and depressed.

As time went on, I felt more and more of a desire to commit suicide. It was not the first time the feeling came over me. I remember vividly: I was home from work early and decided to bathe. I sat there and consumed almost an entire bottle of cough syrup. I was about to consume some pills, but I heard God tell me, "STOP!" The enemy began to tell me suicide was the best way to get over the shame, but God saw me differently. See, the enemy attempts to bombard your mind with negative thoughts to make you feel ugly, unworthy, fearful, pained, and angry.

"Anxiety in the heart of man causes depression, but a good word makes it glad."
(Proverbs 12:25, NKJV)

My husband never left me. Instead, he began to ask what he had done to cause the state of our marriage. As our conversations began to grow, healing and forgiveness began to take place. We did opposite of what the enemy wanted. I started diving into the love of God and began a young women's ministry. I was able to work with ladies who were looking for the love of God. I still didn't know my full potential of God's plan in my life.

A year later, we found out we were expecting our first child. Our marriage wasn't perfect, but we were making progress together. I prayed and sought God for me to be the best mother and wife. During this time, the enemy continued to war against my mind, not allowing me to let go of the brokenness and guilt, but I did not allow it to overtake my mind, marriage, and or pregnancy. My pregnancy was beautiful. I didn't have any complications, and I gave birth to a healthy son.

The following year, I started having symptoms of being pregnant again. I took three home pregnancy tests, which all came back negative. Even the test given by my son's pediatrician was negative. I thought nothing of it…until the day after Mother's Day in May 2012. I was so excited at the thought of going to work that Monday to tell everyone Kaleb had given me the BEST Mother's Day gift by walking! What I thought would be a normal day at work ended up being a nightmare. After being at work for about an hour, I started having really bad stomach pains. I went to the bathroom and noticed I was bleeding. Fear began to overtake me because I didn't know what was going on. I went to my office and fell to the floor in pain and nauseous. I called my husband and my OB/GYN. They told me to come in immediately.

My husband picked me up and, when we arrived at the doctor's, I was engulfed with fear and crying uncontrollably. My doctor ordered an ultrasound and discovered I was bleeding internally. They conducted another pregnancy test; it was still negative. My doctor was uncertain of the cause of the bleeding, so I had to get a CAT Scan and bloodwork. I was so scared and in pain. I began to pray.

Once the results came back, the doctor informed me I was at least five weeks pregnant, but it was an ectopic pregnancy that caused my right tube to burst and bleed internally. I had to undergo emergency surgery immediately. I remember not having time to process any of the emotions between finding out I was pregnant, while having a miscarriage at the same time. As they began to prep me for surgery, my mother-in-law came and got my son. I thought I would never see my husband, son, or family again. I thought I was SURELY going to die.

After the surgery—which was successful—the doctor explained that he couldn't save the tube and my chances of getting pregnant again would be difficult. Emotionally, I felt okay; that was until I had to go back to work and people began asking me if I was okay. I finally broke down and immediately got the doctor to approve my taking a week off. During that week, guilt and depression started to creep their way in.

The enemy told me it was my fault.

The enemy told me I caused the miscarriage.

The enemy told me I deserved what I got.

The enemy told me I would never get pregnant again.

I was broken.

Through the prayers of my husband and a church member who had experienced several miscarriages before birthing two children, I began to believe that God was the final authority. A year and a half later, I found out I was pregnant with my second child. From the beginning, my doctor put me on high risk. I stayed faithful to the Word and knew God was the final authority. I didn't allow any negative thoughts to overtake me.

In February 2014, I gave birth to my daughter. I had no complications. I was taken off high risk alert before my second trimester. God showed Himself mighty and fashioned it in a way that only HE would get the glory.

"For God, who said, "Let light shine out of darkness", is the One who has shone in our hearts to give us the Light of knowledge of the glory and majesty of God [clearly revealed] in the face of Christ."
(2 Corinthians 4:6, AMP)

Slowly, as years passed, I began to open up to my husband about the brokenness and guilt I was still feeling. I allowed God to truly come into my heart because I knew I could not be the best mother and wife unless I was whole. To this day, I have to renew my mind daily.

"Do not be conformed to this world, but be transformed by the renewing of your mind. Then you will be able to discern what is that good, pleasing, and perfect will of God."
(Romans 12:2, NKJV)

In 2015, God told me how to be a wife according to His Word. My purpose was finally revealed! My husband and I began to walk together as heirs of the Kingdom. I began to understand the meaning of being a "Virtuous Woman". True love of myself started to take place.

I published my first book where God revealed to me that its purpose will create divorce-proof marriages. People will understand the true meaning of dating on purpose and respecting the roles God put in place for the family. God never abandoned me. He was there the entire time, waiting and knocking for me to surrender my life to Him.

"Behold, I stand at the door and knock. If anyone hears my voice and opens the door, I will come in to him and dine with him, and he with Me."
(Revelation 3:30, NKJV)

Dr. Minister Mary Faison is a resident of Greensboro, North Carolina, a wife of 23 years to Gene Faison, mother of three, and a proud grandmother. She has served at Daughter of the Embassy Church International for over 16 years under Bishop A.Q. Knotts. She has served in numerous capacities in the ministry. Mary is a licensed Cosmetologist and Makeup Artist. She enjoys helping others feel and look good. She completed her Chaplain certification and is excited about her new journey. She enjoys sewing, meeting people, and traveling.

MY SOMEDAY IS TODAY
Dr. Min. Mary Faison

The future is mine for the taking. How many times have I said that to myself or heard others use those same words with enthusiasm to take control of the future? I wake up one day and realize the 'Future' has become 'Someday'. The future date for the goal to be achieved is someday. We all know 'Someday' is NOT a day of the week, right?

Someday, things will get better.

Someday, I'll eat right.

Someday, I'll have financial freedom.

Someday, I'll have the business I want.

Someday…Someday…Someday…

I had to tell myself that someday is not a day. Someday will always be the same, never allowing me to reach my goals because I gave them to someday with no time in mind, no end date, and no future. We do this and say it so frequently, we believe 'Someday' will happen.

Stop the madness! Learn to live now. That's what I had to do, while believing in myself, but mostly believing in God. I knew God had more and better things for me in my life. I guarded my words with life, not death; speaking to change my world to what I want to see.

God said that I am the head, not the tail. God said He will shower me with favor. I am blessed. Whatever I put my hand to will excel in Jesus' name. I thank Him.

I am…

"For which I am an ambassador in chains that therein I may speak boldly as I ought to speak."
(Ephesians 6:20, KJV)

I am…

Who I am is a child of God.

I am beautiful.

I am healthy.

I am wealthy.

I am loyal.

I am successful.

I am smart.

I am a business woman.

I am great.

I am intelligent.

I am respectful.

I am relaxed.

I am unstoppable.

I am mighty.

I am the best.

I am love.

"Beloved, let us love one another; for love is of God; and everyone that loveth is born of God, and knoweth God."
(1 John 4:7, KJV)

I am worthy because of God.

I am above.

I am strong.

I am loved.

"For God so loved the world, that He gave His Only Begotten Son, that whosoever believeth in Him should not perish, but have everlasting life."
(John 3:16, KJV)

Dare to be happy! I am happy. Do things that make you happy. Be you—original in who God made you to be—and you will be the best you. Happiness comes from the outside. Happiness is determined by the external and what happens to you. We all look different, walk different, act different, and talk like no one else. The worst thing you can do is compare yourself with someone, so don't.

I am joy…

Joy can fill our hearts no matter what is going on in our lives I had to learn to have joy. Joy comes from within.

"May the God of hope fill you with all joy and peace as you trust in Him, so that you may overflow with hope by the power of the Holy Spirit."
(Romans 15:13, KJV)

I am sunshine

I am brave.

I am a flower.

I am a leader.

I am a star.

I am fearless.

I am thoughtful.

Thoughts become things. The Word of God states, 'Set your mind on things that are above'. If you are always saying and thinking things such as, "I don't feel or look good", "I'll never get out of debt", "As soon as things change, things will get better", or "I am always broke", we must remember: *"For as a man thinketh in his heart, so is he"* (Proverbs 23:7, KJV). We have the power over our thoughts. Think of greatness and of God's supernatural blessings and love.

Pastor Cassandra Elliott, also known as the "Purpose Pusher" and the "Giant Slayer", is a walking example of the Five-Fold Ministry. A native of New York City, Elliott began playing music at a young age. This passion unfolded into accepting the call as a Pastor of Worship, teaching the Word of God, and becoming an Innovator and Mentor to many. She is a survivor of Kidney Disease and Breast Cancer, and has used both of these testimonies as a vehicle to encourage other through the preached, taught, and imparting Word of God. In 2016, Elliott launched out into the world of Periscope, launching "Morning Manna"—a time of real talk, inspiration, and coaching. Most recently, Elliott launched out again into the arena of coaching with her debut of Elliott Consulting, which allows clients to come under her mentorship and guidance through various trainings, individual and group coaching internationally. Pastor Cassandra Elliott states, "When we are doing the RIGHT thing with the RIGHT people in the RIGHT place, we will achieve the RIGHT RESULTS!", and God constantly and consistently achieves that through her!

FROM TRAGEDY TO TRIUMPH: MY LIFE OF FAITH
Pastor Cassandra Elliott

What do you do when there has been triumph but now, there is tragedy? What do you do when you come out of chaos into a place of peace and rest, but tragedy shows up again? What do you do?

I remember the day I found "it". I remember the day so very vividly...

I had just finished ministering in praise and worship at a local church as a guest, and I found "it". I don't know what made me do it, but I felt my chest, and there was a lump. It was at the top of my breast and very, very small. It wasn't there earlier that morning. I know it! I would have felt it! It was not there!

After having to do 12 years of peritoneal dialysis—now transplanted eight years—it has been a joy to be out of the season of affliction and now, into a season of rest. God is so amazing. My creatinine was at a perfect 0.8. The doctors were so amazed at how well my body responded to the kidney transplant. This miracle. This answered prayer. Praying for 12 years! Believing God to give me a miracle, and He did. A young lady walked into a conference and told me that God told her to give me a kidney. Not only was she a kidney donor, she was a perfect match—something only God could do. I was in the right place, at the right time, and doing the right thing to receive what God had promised me. I was obedient that night and walked into the conference. I just knew I had to get there.

Bishop Ellis had brought out a Christmas tree in the middle of the week. He said, "God is going to give us Christmas in May! There is going to be a miracle this week." That night, as I went to give an offering, they called me out. They said, "This young lady who serves in ministry here needs a kidney." They began to pray and believe God with me. What a day! Not only did I receive one kidney that night, but three kidneys that same night! Others who knew I needed a kidney came forth to offer their kidney to me!

This will always be my testimony: God keeps His promises. Forever, His Word is settled in Heaven, and He keeps His covenant to His children.

See, you can only imagine how I felt when that lump began to grow. I was traveling in ministry, and the lump continued to grow. You can imagine the questions: "What's going on?" "Why is this happening to me?" "Why now, after coming out of such a time of trial into triumph?" So, I continued to minister, travel, and pray.

Soon, the lump began to grow larger, so I knew I had to make an appointment with my doctor. My doctor knew my history of renal failure, and when I spoke to him about the lump, he said, "It can't be cancer! It can't be!" He knew all I had been through and was hoping and wishing that it was just an infection. He sent me to the breast center to have it drained, thinking it was just something simple. When I arrived, they diagnosed it as "just an infection", prescribed antibiotics, and sent me on my way. To my surprise, they diagnosed it as an infection, but prescribed the wrong medication.

I returned to the doctor two weeks later, only for the doctor to ask for more X-rays to view the lump. At this point, she became very, very concerned and made a decision in a moment. I had no time to pray. I had no time to call to my husband, who was approximately 300 feet away from me behind a door sitting in the lobby waiting for me. She said to me, "Miss Elliott, I need to do a biopsy. Will you allow me to do a biopsy?" I replied, "Yes". She went on to explain it was not an infection and that whatever it was, it was in the tissue of my breast and she couldn't drain it.

As she began to numb the area, I turned my head to the side and silently cried. As the tears began to roll down my face, she handed me a tissue. She knew this was not an easy decision, but it had to happen. It was a very painful procedure, even though she had numbed the area. All I could do was lay there asking God, "What is going on? Why is this happening to me right now? Have I not been through enough?" After she finished the biopsy, she told me she would have the pathology in less than 24 hours. In less than 24 hours, I found out I had breast cancer. As I stood in the doctor's office in the pink robe, I buried my head in my husband's chest and cried. He had to dress me.

I walked through the lobby with my head up. When I got to the car, all I could do was sigh. I knew I had to tell my family. I want to encourage you: Even in the midst of tragedy, God is still the God of Triumph!

After going through six rounds of chemo, losing my hair and strength, I still trusted that God was the God who healed according to **Isaiah 53:4-5**. If He did it before, He would do it again.

Something so amazing happened. When I told my Pastor, he simply asked me, "Cassandra, when do you want this to be over?" I replied, "December". It was August, but I knew I had to go through it. You can't talk about faith and not live faith.

I remember during this time, every morning getting into the presence of God, laying on my face, calling on His name, and believing that He was able. Afterwards, I would go to my keyboard and worship in His presence, singing to Him. There was a song I wrote that simply said, "Strength and courage are what I need from you, Lord. Will you guide my feet and help me? Take my hand and guide me through it all. As long as You are with me, I know everything's going to be alright". I would sit there playing the keyboard with my bald head…

I'll never forget the day I went to the salon and all the ladies who love me showed up as my locs were cut off. One student sat in front at my feet. All of them prayed and held my hands. I could see and feel the Lord giving me strength and courage. That was the day I saw love in action, and although it wasn't easy, God surrounding me with people of faith helped me know I would come through it.

God did so many amazing things during this time. The oncologist could not understand where the lump came from and what was going on, but the mind of God was at work. The oncologist had to call my transplant doctor, and they were able to work together to diagnose my condition. An oncologist and nephrologist had come together to work on my case. What they found out was that they kidney transplant medication has a side effect that caused cancer. My condition was called Post-Transplant Lymphatic Disorder. God wrought the minds of two doctors together to solve my case. Only God! The medication that was supposed to keep my kidney safe had now caused my body to be in trauma. BUT GOD!

I want to let you know that after the second round of chemo, the lump was gone—but I had to go through six rounds of chemo. I was diagnosed cancer-free in January 2014. It was not easy, but it took my level of trust and worship to another dimension. God has not allowed any of my trials to be private. They were made to be public to increase the faith of those who need to believe that God is able.

I have learned to trust God in tragedy and in knowing that *He that began a good work in me is faithful to complete it*. It may seem that my life could have been broken, but thanks be to THE ONE who knows how to put all the pieces back together again!

Tawana T. Valentine Sampson enjoys writing, researching, music, reading, and inspiring others. A native of Rocky Mount, North Carolina, this mother of five moved her family to Greensboro, North Carolina in 1999 after Hurricane Floyd for a better life. Starting at the age of 17 in the telemarketing field, Tawana has since amassed over 30 years of valuable business experience. She has received numerous sales awards and is a 1992 KFC Award winner for song writing. Her research received national recognition in 2014 and was used by non-profit organizations from North Carolina to California to create vision programs to provide residents with free eyeglasses. She is also Community Leader, Civil Rights Activist, and Advocate for humanity. In full force, Tawana is currently a Campaign Ambassador for Nspire Network for the Now We No Awareness Campaign, partnering to inform people all over the world of the harmful effects of traditional sanitary napkin and tampon products. Diagnosed with cancer cells at an early age, Tawana spreads good news about healthy product alternatives, while helping combat the condition of women suffering in silence. You can visit her website at padsstore.com.

PRESSURE BUSTS PIPES
Tawana T. Valentine Sampson

I did not always love myself. My skin is dark, and I grew up thinking black is ugly. The reason I hated being dark-skinned was because I was bullied by someone. From childhood to my high school years, that person called me 'black' on a regular basis, having others join in. As I blossomed, men would tell me how beautiful I was, and I always responded, "Stop lying to me". **Now** I know that black is beautiful. It's actually my favorite color now. This year, I reached out to the person who bullied me for closure. He told me he doesn't remember, but he still apologized. Apology accepted.

When I was 17, I got sick and could barely walk. My parents literally held me up to take me to the doctor. After tests, we found out I had a Urinary Tract Infection and cancer cells. How in the world could a 17-year-old have cancer cells? Thank God, the biopsy came back negative. I didn't understand any of it, but it all makes sense now. I will explain later.

Soon after that episode, I became pregnant. My child's father walked away. I was frowned on. My friends shunned me after seeing other students staring at me and whispering to each other. They didn't want to be 'bothered' with me anymore; however, there were a few people encouraging me. Someone had the audacity to tell me they hoped my baby died. Well, that is what almost happened.

On July 3, 1987, I visited my aunt in Washington, DC. Our church had a convention there. On July 4th, I woke up in a puddle of water. I thought I was dreaming. After the paramedics arrived, they said I had accidentally urinated. I went through the entire day leaking until I saw my cousin (who worked at the hospital) after church that night. Immediately, they took me to Walter Reed Army Hospital. I was a terrified young mother, but I had faith that whatever God was going to do, it was going down.

The nurse stuck me about 10 times trying to put the IV in, and it pissed me off. My body was extremely dehydrated. Then, she delivered the power bomb: I was in labor. "No! No! No!" I cried out to God. "It's too early!" The doctor came in the room and proceeded to tell me that what the nurse had administered to me should slow down the contractions. It didn't work. I was in labor at seven months. He also told me that my baby probably wouldn't survive if it came out alive. I was in disbelief. I looked at my sister, crying and praying. She had to leave me and head back to North Carolina. I was both terrified and alone.

After the delivery, the nurse took my child to the Intensive Care Unit (ICU). I didn't want them to tell me anything. I went into an immediate depression to the point where the nurses told me days after that if I didn't go and visit the baby, it would surely die from not feeling my touch. Finally, I gathered up the strength to go. It was one of the scariest things I had ever done.

Looking at my child—an IV stuck into my baby's head, plastic over that tiny body, and a big, bright light shining from above on my child—brought tears to my eyes. It was a sight to see. My child weighed 1 lb., 8 oz. with a 50% chance of living.

I prayed, "God, if this child is to live, let it live. If this child is to die, that's Your will."

I left the ICU in peace.

My mother came to visit me at the hospital, and we were called to the Administrator's office for them to deliver the bill. It was $75,000.00! I almost passed out! I knew we didn't have the money to pay for the hospital bill. "Ma'am, I'm 17 years old. How am I supposed to pay for this?" She quaintly said, "I don't know". My mother went OFF and said, "If 21 years of my husband serving doesn't pay for it, you won't be getting it!" We left the office.

I had to go back home for school and leave my child behind. About a month later, I got a phone call stating that heart surgery had to be performed on my child. At that point, there was a 33% chance of living. I was tired and still worried while having to give an authorization over the telephone to move forward.

I couldn't focus on school, and my grades had dropped. Another bomb shell was delivered from the principal. I got kicked out of school for missing too many days. Teachers and students cried along with me.

Today, my child is 30 years old and healthy.

That experience took my belief in God to a whole different level.

In 2007, I was a Senior Mortgage Loan Officer and Processor. I was no longer on public assistance and was taking care of five children. It was such an honor to call and tell Social Services to cut me off!

My family lived in a very beautiful two-story home. It was so nice that the police showed up one day because someone said they thought we were breaking in. I had to show the police our lease. We had a basketball court and a huge yard with a gazebo. I was driving my dream vehicle: a Chevy Suburban. Life was great!

At the peak of my career, my paycheck was over $40,000.00 for one month. Then, the housing market crashed! One by one, my loans were denied. I had no money saved up. I started hearing stories from my Account Executives and other Loan Officers about people losing their luxuries, like yachts and penthouses. I knew it was just a matter of time for my family and me. Eventually, we were homeless.

We moved to a roach-infested, raunchy hotel for about two months. We were then able to move across the street to a better hotel for almost a year. While there, the time came for me to renew my mortgage license for $50.00 or lose it. It was either pay the weekly hotel rent or lose my license with nowhere for us to go. I chose to lose my license.

That was a very stressful time, but I bounced back for a bit and then was homeless again, living in a hotel for another year. It's funny because as I was washing clothes one day at the second hotel while standing in the laundry room looking at the clothes wash, I heard a voice say, *"You are going to write a book of all the traumas that you have survived to uplift others"*. I chalked it up to my mind tripping; yet here I am, telling you some of my story! One of my high school teachers had already told me that I'd be a great writer. Life is funny.

My whole life has been changed for the better from what I have been through. Recently, I have been studying the Law of Attraction, meditating, and doing Chakra exercises, along with prayer. I'm into sowing good seeds because I know those seeds must grow. My practices are paying off generously. How, you might ask? Well, I'm glad you asked!

Two weeks ago, I went to the Waffle House and placed my order. The waitress put in one meal; I received two. On another day, I went to a restaurant, ordered a large pizza, and got one for free. The same week, I went to another restaurant and got about $15.00 worth of free food because they got my order wrong and told me to keep what I had. It's the small things we should be grateful for, and more great things will happen for us. Last week, I moved and have a swimming pool on my vision board. By the way, I also have my mortgage license back.

Okay. Now, back to the cancer cell story. It is 31 years later, and I am in full force, being a leader and activist with *Now We No Awareness Campaign*—a campaign informing women and men all over the world about the harmful effects today's sanitary napkins and tampons may have on women's bodies. The *Now We No Movement* will partner with women's organizations and cancer awareness groups in the United States and internationally. For more information, visit www.noweno.net and www.nspirenetwork.com/tawanasampson.

Life has dealt me some raggedy cards like the dolls, but I dance to my own beat. Dance to your own beat. Be grateful through the good and the bad. You will make it to your destination. It might take days, months, or even years, but keep dancing!

Stay focused!

Be inspired!

Montell McClain was born and raised in Rocky Mount, North Carolina. She was an early childhood professional before shifting to writing, humanitarianism, and motivational speaking. She currently resides in Raleigh, North Carolina and is the mother of four wonderful adult children and two amazing grandchildren. Montell has an Associate's Degree in Early Childhood Education from Wake Technical Community College in Raleigh, North Carolina and a Bachelor's Degree in Child Development with a Specialization in Infant/Toddler from Walden University. She is also a member of the nation's largest Honor Society, Sigma Alpha Pi, the National Society of Leadership and Success. Her church home is Crossroads Fellowship in Raleigh. Montell has a loving heart. She is currently working on starting a non-profit organization for disadvantaged individuals, helping to pave a way to a brighter future. She also has a love for reading and is working on coordinating a family literary program. She's hoping that one of the many children's books she has written will be on the shelves in her program.

ABANDONMENT
Montell McClain

"Can a woman forget her nursing child, that she should have no compassion on the son of her womb? Even these may forget, yet I will not forget you."
(Isaiah 49:15, NKJV)

Early in life, I began having feelings of uncertainty. My parents divorced when I was a little girl, and I was reared by my father and his family. I was loved and cared for, but I still felt as if I did not belong. I felt there was something missing in my life and like a puzzle piece that did not fit anywhere. The enemy tried to apprehend me with depression. I battled the depression and the feelings of worthlessness, loneliness, and low self-esteem.

These years brought on major weight gain, and I lost control of my life. During this time, I would go into isolation. I remember so vividly when my children were small, I would close the blinds so no light could enter the house. I would turn off the ringer of the phone so I couldn't receive phone calls, while my children sat in front of the television with the volume down low. I separated myself from those who wanted to be in my life, all because of those who left me. The negative thoughts of the enemy would plummet my mind all the time. I was broken and had been hurt by so many people. This cycle continued because I was being disobedient to Christ. I was not on the path He had created for me.

Living life outside of His will caused me to sustain excruciating pain. The pain inflicted was by those who I considered personal and close friends. The others who inflicted pain were family. The pain I experienced had seared my heart and soul. The continuous nightmare of being a motherless child, searching to be a part of someone's life caused me to rummage immensely and effortlessly for love. I have been cheated on, lied on, lied to, mistreated, and shunned. Not many can endure blow after blow after blow. I had to turn away from my carnal mind and this ungodly world, and seek the face of our Almighty God.

Even though I was breaking down, torn up and worn out, I had to pick up the pieces and hand them to God. God made me whole again. He had already paid the price for me, and He graciously accepted me into His Kingdom. He healed my brokenness and gave me the insurmountable, unconditional love I desperately sought after. God allowed me to take the broken pieces of my life and construct a platform so that I can speak of His goodness, His grace, and His never-ending mercy.

Jeremiah 29:11 (NIV) states, *"For I know the plans I have for you, declares the Lord; plans to prosper you and not to harm you, plans to give you hope and a future"*. I discerned that this is my season. I now align myself with Christ and bold into the course that He has for my life. I hold on to the handrail of God, step on the head of abandonment, and upsurge to the next level of my life.

In Acts 4:32 (AMP), we find: *"And the multitude of them that believed were of one heart and of one soul: neither said any [of them] that ought of the things which he possessed was his own; but they had all things in common."* I had spent years with my soul emotionally tied to things and to the wrong people. At one point in my life, I devoted myself and was passionate about a career that I loved. I tied my soul to that work and those children, and I was wrongfully and unprofessionally removed my position. For months, I was broken. I was hurt. I lost my passion and wanted those who wrongfully maltreated me to feel the pain I felt. I no longer wanted to work again. I felt deceived.

One night, I got down on my knees and prayed to God. I said, "Father, please help me. Contend, Lord, with those who contend with me. Fight against those who fight against me, God. Let them know that all things work together for good to them that love You, to them who are called according to Your purpose".

I pursued after a love that only God could bestow. I wanted to be the love of someone's life, to be that piece that was missing from their heart. I experienced relationships where I copulated and was subsequently riddled with guilt. My soul tied to an individual deeply and emotionally. I would battle with their soul and the souls of those they had tied themselves to. I can remember voicing my truthful thoughts and feelings and my carnal desires, only to be left broken I repetitively tied my soul to barren, meaningless relationships. I hold on to the handrail of God, step on the head of those soul ties, and rise to the next level of my life.

> *"Brethren, I count not myself to have apprehended: but this one thing I do, forgetting those things which are behind, and reaching forth unto those things which are before. I press toward the mark for the prize of high calling of God in Christ Jesus."*
> (Philippians 3:13-14, NKJV)

I hold on tightly to the handrail of God. He lifts me up as I take each step towards the next level in my life. I may have started out carrying a lot of baggage, but most of the bags have fallen off along the way: the bag of abandonment; the bag seeking fleshly love; the baggage of guilt, depression, and shame; and the baggage of family and friends who were only meant to be in my life for a season.

I have gathered that if I am not walking in the will of God, I will undergo discomfort and anxiety. I will feel out of place. I will not fit in because I was meant to stand out. I will not like my job because my Father planned for me to be an entrepreneur. I hold on to the handrail of God as He lifts me up. My Father has prepared a way for me. He has given me the mighty gift of discernment and has made those transparent who wish to do me harm. He has encircled me with His fiery hedge of protection and has placed angels all around me as I hold on to His hand.

From the broken pieces of my life, I will build a platform. I will rise to speak of His goodness, His grace, and His never-ending mercy.

"That if thou shalt confess with thy mouth the Lord Jesus, and shalt believe in thine heart that God hath raised Him from the dead, thou shalt be saved."
(Romans 10:9, KJV)

God saved me from myself. He delivered me from those thoughts of worthlessness and from the oppressed spirit. If you just believe, He can do the same for you. Our God is much larger than any problem we may go through. He is a way-maker and an on-time God. There were times when I would cry and call out to my Heavenly Father, but even as I lay in silence, I heard nothing. I would think He had abandoned me, but I gained the wisdom to know that the teacher is quiet during the test. Through wisdom, I have learned that our Heavenly Father protects us the same way as our earthly father would. If our earthly father sees us about to run out into traffic, he will rush to our aid and redirect us. The same goes for our Heavenly Father. The people we miss and want in our lives, God removed them and interceded in those relationships to protect us. Their seasons in our lives are over.

"And be not conformed to this world: but be ye transformed by the renewing of your mind, that ye may prove what is that good, and acceptable, and perfect will of God."
(Romans 12:2, KJV)

I pick up my broken pieces, one by one. I build a platform so that I can confess the goodness of my Lord and Savior, Jesus Christ, and all that He has done for me. If He can do it for me, He can—and He will—do it for you. I may become weary as I travel through my temporary home on earth, but I will still hold on to His hand. When I am tired, I will look to Him to regain the strength I need to keep pressing towards the mark. By His stripes, I am healed. I love and forgive as I step onto my platform.

Cynthia Randolph is the Founder of *Cater To You Incorporated, LLC*. Cynthia established *Cater To You Incorporated, LLC* in 2012 and offers wedding/event planning and organizing support to individuals, business owners, and entrepreneurs. Her greatest strengths are her creativity, drive, and leadership. She thrives on challenges, particularly those that expand the company's reach. Cynthia has worked with clients in many different states. She does not limit her event-planning technique. She is versatile and adjusts with her clients' needs. Cynthia uses her life's experience to ensure her clients' needs are met.

ALL OF THE PIECES WERE NECESSARY
Cynthia Randolph

As I look back over my life and journey, I see where I have left pieces of myself over the years. I am loving how I am now taking those missing pieces and fitting them together as the platform I will continue to stand on and be proud of. Without the missing pieces, things, and what I have been through, I wouldn't be the person I am today.

My first piece of my platform was formed during my pre-teen years when I took the pain from that part of my life and learned how to hide my pain easily. In the long run, I also set myself up for future disappointment and, subsequently, set the stage for the next piece of my platform to be formed.

The next piece of my platform was formed during my teens, and it was a difficult piece; one full of hurt, disappointment, betrayal, and my asking, "Why am I even here on this earth?" I even contemplated ending my life, but I had a friend who talked to me about why I shouldn't. That same friend told me to reach out if I ever had that feeling again because there was more to life than ending it over a few bumps in the road.

The next piece of my platform was shaped in my 20s: I had my first child. I knew I wasn't going to raise him with the help of his father, but I was happy to have my family in my corner. It was this strength and love that helped me get through this part of my life and a lot of the trials and bumps in the road to come.

In my 30s, the next piece of my platform was formed. Yes, this was definitely the roughest part of my journey, when my faith and strength was truly tested the most. I met my future husband and was looking to my future business endeavor. During this time, I also lost my grandparents who I spent my life around. It hurt me so much. Still, I had to be strong for my mother, if for nothing or anything else. I still had moments when I stopped and thought of what my life had become. I knew there was so much more to it to make this journey worth it every day.

In this next piece of my life, my 40s, I am taking all of my previous pieces and holding them together with faith, strength, and wisdom. I will use them for my platform as fuel to help push me to move my business forward and upward. These pieces will continue to move me towards my vision for my lie and serve my children as a legacy. I know women who have gone through hell and back, but they didn't make it out fine at all. Then, there are those who have made it and are champions, reaching back to help other women through the fire. I want to be one of those women who is reaching back and bringing the next woman through her fire.

Now,
YOU continue on building your own platform!

LOVING THE LIFE I LIVE, LLC
AND THE AUTHORS OF
THE PIECES OF MY PLATFORM
WOULD LIKE TO THANK OUR SPONSORS.
WITHOUT EACH OF YOU, THIS PROJECT WOULD NOT HAVE BEEN POSSIBLE.
"THANK YOU!"

SPONSORS

Ida M. Robinson
Mom Empowerment Coach
https://momnpowerment.com
Ida@momnpowerment.com

Kim Urban
Nerium Health and Wellness Products
www.ndakku.nerium.com

Shiryl Butler
Paparazzi Jewelry & Accessories
Independent Consultant
www.paparazziaccessories.com/64444

Carol Mortarotti
Grief Recovery Healer
forgiveandconquer.com/

Wendy Magee
Author | Speaker | Founder of Speak Up Ministry
www.wendymagee.org

LaShinya Davis
Traci Lynn Jewelry
Independent Consultant
www.tracilynnjewelry.net/17098

Dominique D Jones
Breaking Through The Silence (Organization)
www.ilivesoyoucan.simplesite.com

Dr. Sharon H. Porter
Perfect Time SHP LLC
Coaching and Consulting Firm
www.PerfectTimeSHP.com

Dr. Sharon H. Porter
The GRIND Entrepreneur Network
www.theGRINDeNetwork.com

Dr. Sharon H. Porter
Write the Book Now! Aspiring Author's Weekend Retreat
www.WritetheBookNow.com

Dr. Sharon H. Porter,
Educator | Author | Speaker
www.SharonHPorter.com

Coretta Campbell
Jewelry Stylist
Traci Lynn Jewelry
www.tracilynnjewelry.net/3421

Rachel White
Certified Life Coach | Public Speaker | Author
Disciples of the Blood of the Lamb Outreach Ministries, Inc.
www.disciplesoftheblood.org

Carmen Ring
Translator
I help entrepreneurs expand their brand internationally. Not just by translating their content, but also designing strategies to get them visible on new and unfamiliar markets
CARMENRING.COM

Jasmine Berkley
Helping Hands Travel Agency
Independent Artist
www.protravelnetwork.com/jasmineberkley

Simply Unique Breaking the Silence
www.simplyuniquebts.com
Inspirational Speaker / Advocate Against Sexual Violence

Derek Palmer, Owner
Derek Palmer Photography
http://www.derekpalmerphotography.com/

L.A. Photography
www.luguzyphotos.com/

Deloris Williams, CEO
Divine Connections Magazine
www.divineconnections.info

Lateka S Carter
Manager and Founder
Kingdom Designing Production, LLC
transitionyouin90days.com

Sathya Callender Nelson, Owner
Kutie Patooties ("All Things Made Beautiful")
www.kutiepatootie.com

Kia Stewart
Artist | Singer | Songwriter | Promoter
www.kiastewart.com

Diane P. Rembert
Diamond's Literary World
www.diamondsliteraryworld.com

Duane Nash
Cover Designer for "The Pieces of My Platform"
Graphic Designer
designnash@gmail.com

Tijuana Smith-Realtor
Caldwell Banker
704dreamhomes.com

Portia Shipman, Founder/Executive Director
Sherri Denese Jackson Foundation
sdjfnc.org

Adrian Martinca – Personal Laptop Scholarships K-12
Technology for the Future (A Community Partners Program)
technologyforthefuture.org

Rev. Nelson and Joyce Johnson
The Beloved Community Center
www.belovedcommunitycenter.org

Five Point Tax Service, Inc.
116 Greensboro Rd
High Point, NC 27260
Office (336) 885-4244

Dwayne Rogers
Nairobi Professional Hair Care-B & G Distributing
(336) 419-8546

Crystal Williams-Owner
House of Nutrition
www.facebook.com/pages/House-of-Nutrition/1570813919881753

Their Faces

PLATFORM BUILDER STEVII AISHA MILLS

PLATFORM BUILDER
PASTOR CASSANDRA ELLIOTT

PLATFORM BUILDER
CYNTHIA RANDOLPH

PLATFORM BUILDER
MARY FAISON

PLATFORM BUILDER LATONYA KNOX

PLATFORM BUILDER TI'KEYA LAWRENCE

PLATFORM BUILDER
ALICIA DIGGS

THE PIECES OF MY PLATFORM

PLATFORM BUILDER
SAN GRIFFIN

PLATFORM BUILDER MINISTER KIESHA PETERSON

PLATFORM BUILDER WENDY MAGEE

PLATFORM BUILDER
TAWANA T. VALENTINE SAMPSON

PLATFORM BUILDER
CAROL CRAVEN

PLATFORM BUILDERS
(Not pictured)

MONTELL McCLAIN

LAVERNE PERSCELL

SHANAWA RICHARDSON

JESSICA ENDENDO

THE PIECES OF MY PLATFORM

ABOUT THE VISIONARY AUTHOR

CEO | SPEAKER | PR & TRAVEL CONSULTANT |
RADIO HOST | BEST-SELLING AUTHOR

Stevii Aisha Mills embraces a culture where fun is not just a niche, it is a necessity! Stevii is a native of Greensboro, North Carolina and a proud graduate of North Carolina A&T State University, where Aggie Pride reigns. Her formal education consists of a B.A. in Public Relations and an M.S. in Human Resources; however, Stevii's real-life experiences have made her a well-known Social Media Influencer and gained her the title "The Chief IT Factor Cultivator"! A woman unashamed to incorporate tons of fun into her life and business, all the while declaring, "I love my life!" has made Stevii a highly sought-out Speaker and Consultant.

Stevii is a true CEO/Founder of the B.E.A.U.T.Y. From Head-to-Toe Tour and the B.E.A.U.T.Y. Queen Society and her anchor company "Just Stevii". She is also the Host of the "The Conversation with Stevii" on iHeart Radio and the Visionary Author of the best-selling book *Cultivating Your IT Factor*. Her entrepreneurial spirit shines brightly when she combines various ventures, such as the marriage of her travel company and conferences and retreats. Stevii is a wiz at combining and comingling various resources and people to create a total life change for all.

As a distinguished Toastmaster, Stevii moves an audience to action as she speaks clarity to their minds and stirs passion in the hearts. Stevii is most often called upon to speak on topics of self-esteem, team-building, success with public relations, and living a healthy and fun-filled lifestyle. As a representative of Total Life Changes ® and World Ventures ®, coupled with a degree in Public Relations, Stevii speaks knowledgeably in each of these topics.

Stevii Aisha Mills is a woman on a mission to increase joy and clarity to the world—one conversation, one vacation, and one experience at a time.

Everyone can rock their IT FACTOR with Stevii in the room!

I'm here to help you ROCK your IT FACTOR in an awesome, dynamic way!

Are you ready?

STEVII AISHA MILLS' ACHIEVEMENTS

- Founder of the B.E.A.U.T.Y. From Head-to-Toe Tour and the B.E.A.U.T.Y. Queen Society.
- Served as the Director of Marketing on the National Board of Directors for Lambda Tau Upsilon Sorority.
- Recognized as the 2011 recipient of the "Rising Star Award", presented at the Rising Stars Concert—a fundraising event for the Janice L. Mills Scholarship Foundation.
- Served as the Marketing Chairperson for the Special Events Ministry at Destiny Christian Center.
- Earned the distinguished title of "Competent Communicator" in Toastmasters International.
- Writer of the world-recognized "Just Stevii" column.
- Host of "The Conversation" Podcast.
- Curated CD entitled "Definition of a B.E.A.U.T.Y. Queen".
- Served as a member of the Leadership Team of The Queen's Foundation and recognized as the Volunteer of the Month in July 2014.
- Successfully completed a Human Resources internship with Walt Disney World Resorts.
- Served as Director of Personal and Business Development for Professional Women Entrepreneurs.

APPENDIX

AVERTing HIV and AIDS. (2017). *HIV Stigma and Discrimination.* Retrieved from https://www.avert.org/professionals/hiv-social-issues/stigmadiscrimination

National Institute of Mental Health. (2016). *Depression*. Retrieved from https://www.nimh.nih.gov/health/topics/depression/index.shtml

www.ingramcontent.com/pod-product-compliance
Lightning Source LLC
Chambersburg PA
CBHW070632300426
44113CB00010B/1746